MONSTER Cranes

by Nick Gordon

BELLWETHER MEDIA · MINNEAPOLIS, MN

Note to Librarians, Teachers, and Parents:

Blastoff! Readers are carefully developed by literacy experts and combine standards-based content with developmentally appropriate text.

Level 1 provides the most support through repetition of high-frequency words, light text, predictable sentence patterns, and strong visual support.

Level 2 offers early readers a bit more challenge through varied simple sentences, increased text load, and less repetition of high-frequency words.

Level 3 advances early-fluent readers toward fluency through increased text and concept load, less reliance on visuals, longer sentences, and more literary language.

Level 4 builds reading stamina by providing more text per page, increased use of punctuation, greater variation in sentence patterns, and increasingly challenging vocabulary.

Level 5 encourages children to move from "learning to read" to "reading to learn" by providing even more text, varied writing styles, and less familiar topics.

Whichever book is right for your reader, Blastoff! Readers are the perfect books to build confidence and encourage a love of reading that will last a lifetime!

This edition first published in 2014 by Bellwether Media, Inc.

No part of this publication may be reproduced in whole or in part without written permission of the publisher. For information regarding permission, write to Bellwether Media, Inc., Attention: Permissions Department, 5357 Penn Avenue South, Minneapolis, MN 55419.

Library of Congress Cataloging-in-Publication Data

Gordon, Nick.
  Monster cranes / by Nick Gordon.
    pages cm. – (Blastoff! readers: Monster machines)
  Summary: "Developed by literacy experts for students in kindergarten through grade three, this book introduces extreme cranes to young readers through leveled text and related photos"–Provided by publisher.
  Audience: K-3
  Includes bibliographical references and index.
  ISBN 978-1-60014-936-8 (hardcover : alkaline paper)
  1. Cranes, derricks, etc.–Juvenile literature. I. Title.
  TJ1363.G6765 2014
  621.8'73–dc23
                                                            2013002285

Table of Contents

Monster Cranes!

Big jobs need
big cranes.
These machines
lift heavy loads.

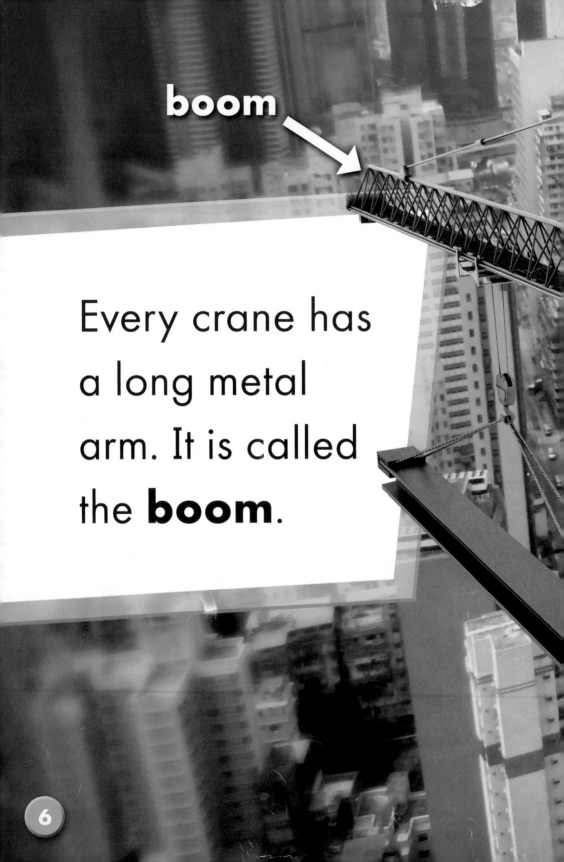

boom

Every crane has a long metal arm. It is called the **boom**.

The boom is often taller than a **skyscraper**!

Cranes on the Move

Many cranes have big wheels or **tracks**. They are **mobile cranes**.

tracks

Some cranes
work from ships.
They are called
floating cranes.

Fixed Cranes

Tower cranes are the tallest. They are **fixed cranes**.

Gantry cranes are also fixed cranes. They help build and load ships.

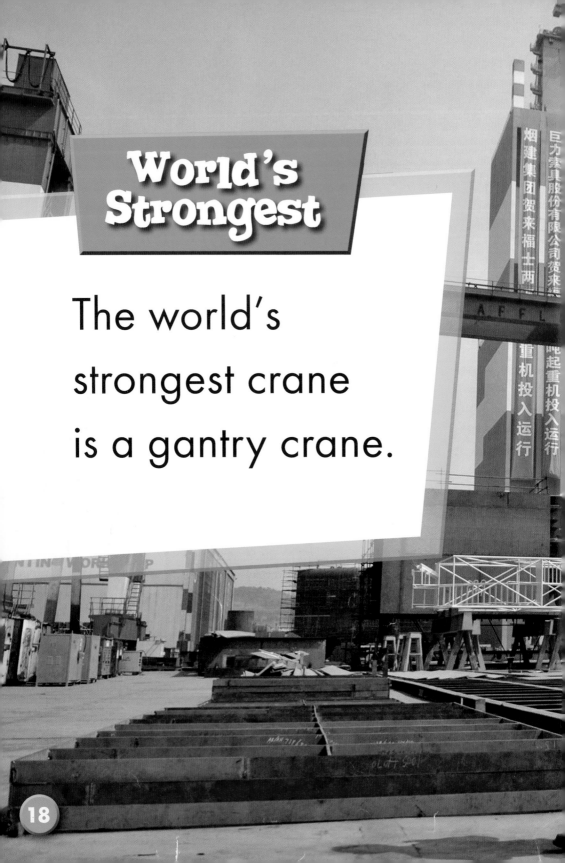

World's Strongest

The world's strongest crane is a gantry crane.

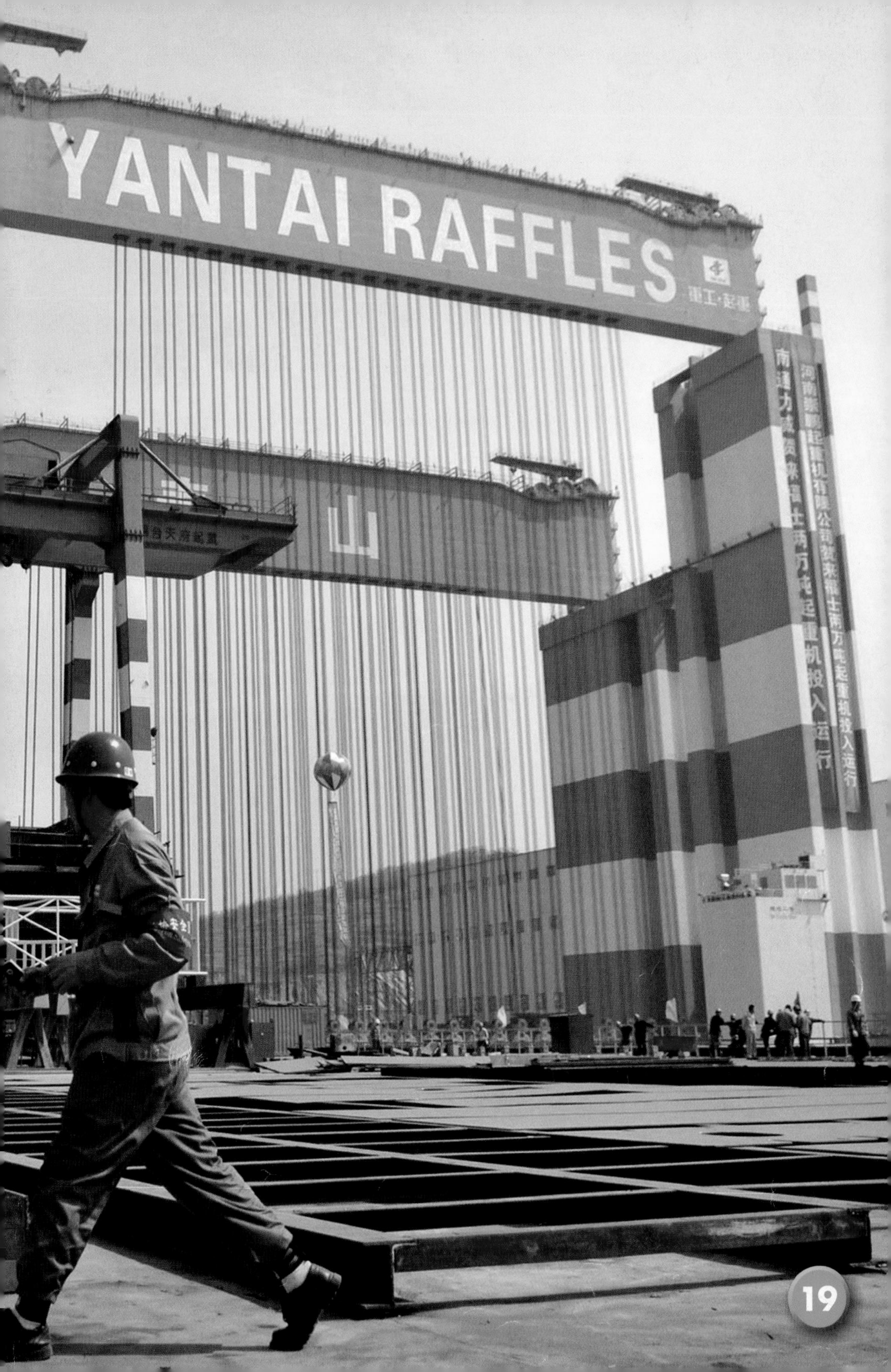
YANTAI RAFFLES

It can lift the weight of 10,000 cars. Wow!

Glossary

boom—the long, moveable arm on a crane

fixed cranes—cranes that stay in one place

gantry cranes—fixed cranes with a lift that is connected to strong metal beams

mobile cranes—cranes that can move from place to place

skyscraper—a very tall building

tower cranes—tall fixed cranes often used to build skyscrapers

tracks—large belts that wrap around wheels; some mobile cranes move on tracks.

To Learn More

AT THE LIBRARY

Addison, D. R. *Cranes at Work*. New York, N.Y.: PowerKids Press, 2009.

Allen, Kenny. *Giant Cranes*. New York, N.Y.: Gareth Stevens Pub., 2013.

Peppas, Lynn. *Cranes*. New York, N.Y.: Crabtree Pub. Co., 2012.

ON THE WEB

Learning more about cranes is as easy as 1, 2, 3.

1. Go to www.factsurfer.com.

2. Enter "cranes" into the search box.

3. Click the "Surf" button and you will see a list of related Web sites.

With factsurfer.com, finding more information is just a click away.

Index